CAREERS ON

ANTITERRORISM & COUNTERTERRORISM TASK FORCES

CAREERS ON

ANTITERRORISM &
COUNTERTERRORISM
TASK FORCES

CORINNE GRINAPOL

ROSEN
PUBLISHING®

New York

Published in 2014 by The Rosen Publishing Group, Inc.
29 East 21st Street, New York, NY 10010

Library of Congress Cataloging-in-Publication Data

Grinapol, Corinne.
Careers on antiterrorism and counterterrorism task forces/Corinne Grinapol.
— First edition.
    pages cm. — (Extreme law enforcement)
Includes bibliographical references and index.
ISBN 978-1-4777-1711-0 (library binding)
1. Terrorism—Prevention—Vocational guidance. I. Title.
HV6431.G7457 2013
363.325'15023—dc23

                                                                2013013751

Manufactured in the United States of America

CPSIA Compliance Information: Batch #W14YA: For further information, contact Rosen
Publishing, New York, New York, at 1-800-237-9932.

CONTENTS

INTRODUCTION

On the evening of May 2, 2011, President Barack Obama appeared on television to make an announcement ten years in the making: Osama bin Laden was dead. In the weeks before the president's announcement, a team of a dozen SEALs from the U.S. Navy's elite counterterrorism force, SEAL Team Six, was told to report for training in the woods of North Carolina. Training is a regular part of a SEAL's life, and the men didn't know when they were called to North Carolina that they were prepping for a mission to take down Osama bin Laden. He was suspected to be living in a compound in Abbottabad, Pakistan. For five days the men trained in the woods, practicing getting into a building built for the occasion: a copy of the real-life compound they would soon be breaking into.

A week of training in the desert of Nevada followed. In Nevada, at night, the

BIN LADEN KILLED BY U.S. FORCES OBAMA SAYS, DECLARING JUSTICE.

VOL. CLX ... No. 55,393

That's Fit to Print

As the leader of Al Qaeda, Osama bin Laden, here in video recorded in 2001, waged a

OSAMA BIN LADEN, 1957-2011

lem of Evil in the U.S., an Ico

Following President Obama's announcement, the front pages of newspapers across the country display the news that Osama bin Laden had been killed by Navy SEALs in Abbottabad, Pakistan.

7

SEALs worked on their fast roping skills, in which they descend rapidly down a rope suspended from a moving helicopter.

The plan for the May 1 mission, called Operation Neptune's Spear, was to fast rope onto the roof of the compound, but when one of the helicopters almost crashed and was forced to land, the SEALs quickly improvised, as their vast mission experience prepared them to do. The SEALs exited the helicopters and ran toward the walls of the compound, using explosives to unlock the gates. Once inside, wearing night vision goggles, armed with pistols, rifles, and maps of the compound, the SEALs made their way toward their main target.

When the SEALs reached bin Laden, he was surrounded by his wives. One of the SEALs used his body to pull away the two women standing in front of bin Laden. The other two SEALs in the room were then able to take their shots. Soon the entire world would know what the SEALs had accomplished. Osama bin Laden, the man who had planned the deadliest attack ever on American soil, was dead.

This is just one very famous example of what a counterterrorism or antiterrorism task force does or can accomplish. The broader picture is more complex, with a varied assortment of forces and available positions on task forces that appeal to people with many different types of minds, interests, and skill sets. It is a world that includes teams that take down the world's most notorious terrorists, teams that do the work of figuring out where the terrorists are, teams that prevent a plot from ever getting off the ground, and teams that figure out how to keep the country safe before a plan against the country ever takes shape.

The following information will help you learn about the available positions on task forces, how to make it on to one of those teams, and the things you can start doing right now that will help get you there.

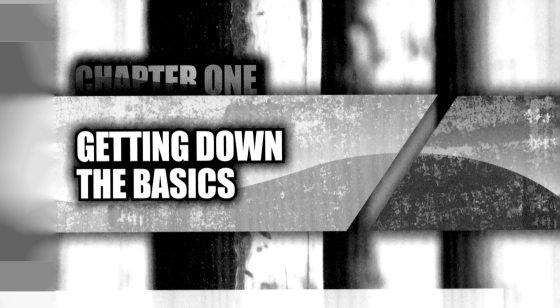

CHAPTER ONE

GETTING DOWN THE BASICS

The form that terrorism has taken has changed over time and most likely will continue to change. Part of the reason there has been such a large diversity of terrorists and terrorist organizations is because there is no single all-encompassing definition of what terrorism is or who is considered a terrorist.

Why a Definition Matters

The U.S. Code, which is the collection of all active laws passed by Congress or found in the U.S. Constitution, defines terrorism as "premeditated, politically motivated violence perpetrated against noncombatant targets by subnational groups or clandestine agents."

According to the code, for an act to be considered terrorism, it has to be planned in advance, be violent, and have a political purpose. In addition, it has to be committed either by an individual or group not representing the government, meaning a violent action by a government would not be considered terrorism. Finally, the target of this action has to be a noncombatant, meaning either a civilian or an off-duty member of the military.

Under this definition, neither of these scenarios would constitute terrorism: a group of heirs who kills a relative to get money from that person's will; a member of a terrorist organization who kills a soldier during a battle. In the first, the reason for the murder is greed, not to send a message. In the second, the soldier is active in battle and isn't considered a noncombatant.

The Department of Defense (DOD), which represents the U.S. military, uses the following definition: "The unlawful use of violence or threat of violence to instill fear and coerce governments or societies. Terrorism is often motivated by religious, political, or other ideological beliefs and committed in the pursuit of goals that are usually political."

The Department of Defense's definition is more expansive than the definition in the U.S. Code. The U.S. Code definition deals with actions that have happened, but the DOD includes in its definition the intention or threat to commit the acts. The DOD definition also adds motives beyond politics. For example, many members of an organization known as the Army of God have undertaken terrorist acts, among them the bombing of abortion clinics. The members of the group claim that god wants them to commit these acts, making the motivations for those acts of violence religious, rather than political.

A member of the Army of God demonstrates during jury selection for the trial of James Kopp, who was accused—and later convicted—of murdering abortion provider

The FBI's definition is "the unlawful use of force or violence against persons or property to intimidate or coerce a government, the civilian population, or any segment thereof, in furtherance of political or social objectives."

The FBI includes attacks against property, not just people, in its definition. For example, on May 18, 2009, the offices of a company known as Scientific Resources International in Nevada were destroyed in a fire. No one was hurt. A group known as the Animal Liberation Front (ALF) took responsibility. The group was opposed to the company sending monkeys to other organizations for use in experiments. According to the FBI definition of terrorism, this constitutes a terrorist act.

Defining Your Future

With all the varying definitions, the possibilities for what constitutes terrorism and who can be considered a terrorist are broad and wide-ranging. This means that many different organizations with different goals and operating procedures have taken on the cause of antiterrorism and counterterrorism, going after different aspects of terrorist activities with different methods.

For those interested in a career in counterterrorism or antiterrorism, this is good news. There are many different career paths that can lead to a job on an antiterrorism or counterterrorism task force. Those interested in a more physically demanding, security-based position can start their careers in the military, as a police officer, or as an FBI agent.

THE ALPHABET SOUP OF COUNTERTERRORISM—A BEGINNER'S GUIDE TO ACRONYMS

Acronyms abound in the fields of counterterrorism and antiterrorism. Below are some more commonly used acronyms.

ABM: Antiballistic missile

AMD: Air and missile defense

AT: Antiterrorism

ATFP: Antiterrorism force protection

CBRN: Chemical, biological, radiological, and nuclear

CI: Counterintelligence

COIN: Counterinsurgency

CT: Counterterrorism

IED: Improvised explosive device

RPG: Rocket-propelled grenade

SCUD: Surface-to-surface missile system

USCENTCOM: U.S. central command

USSTRATCOM: U.S. strategic command

WMD: Weapons of mass destruction

Those who have more academic inclinations can do more analytical work, beginning their careers as intelligence analysts with the CIA or FBI.

There is also plenty of room to specialize in the field since work in counterterrorism and antiterrorism may require special working knowledge of cyber-warfare, dealing with explosives and other dangerous weapons, foreign languages, and the extensive study of different political, religious, and social movements.

Counterterrorism Compared to Antiterrorism

Although the terms appear to be similar, "counterterrorism" (CT) and "antiterrorism" (AT) are by no means interchangeable. According to the *DOD Dictionary of Military Terms*, the definition for antiterrorism is "defensive measures used to reduce the vulnerability of individuals and property to terrorist acts, to include rapid containment by local military and civilian forces. Also called AT."

For counterterrorism it is "actions taken directly against terrorist networks and indirectly to influence and render global and regional environments inhospitable to terrorist networks. Also called CT."

When researching AT and CT task forces, you may discover that these terms are sometimes confused, or are used interchangeably. A news report may, for example, refer to the

Terrorist attacks on American soil tend to result in greater antiterrorism protections in their aftermath. Here, tourists pass through concrete barriers to visit the Washington Monument. Barriers prevent car or truck bombs from reaching targets.

antiterrorism efforts of a task force that has the word "counterterrorism" in its name. Adding to the confusion, some task forces choose to forgo either term, such as the National Joint Terrorism Task Force (NJTTF). It's important to look at the goals and methods the organization uses to combat terrorism; this is where the difference between counterterrorism and antiterrorism becomes clearer.

Antiterrorism's defensive approach focuses on protection, preparation, and training. There is a lot of organizing of programs, people, and places involved. AT task forces focus on making sure those involved in combating terrorism are prepared through education, training, and role-playing.

THE INTELLIGENCE KALEIDOSCOPE

Intelligence comes from a variety of sources, some surprising. The major types of intelligence are:

Human-source intelligence (HUMINT). This is what most people generally associate with intelligence gathering: intelligence that comes from people or is gathered by people. This includes work by undercover, or clandestine, agents from the CIA, but also people like diplomats and military personnel working in other countries who openly collect information in the course of their regular duties.

Open-source intelligence (OSINT). Intelligence gathered from the types of open sources we are exposed to on a daily basis: radio, television, the Internet, newspapers, and even drawings. This is the type of intelligence that demonstrates the need for skillful analysis and interpretation; it relies on the ability to see patterns and clues in everyday things.

Signals intelligence (SIGINT). Intelligence that comes from signals exchanged between people and/or machines. This type of information exchange is often coded and requires decoding and interpretation.

> **Imagery intelligence (IMINT). Intelligence that comes from pictures. This includes photographs, but also pictures of objects taken through radar, infrared, or laser imagery.**
>
> **Measurement and signature intelligence (MASINT). MASINT relies on technologies such as infrared heat imaging and night vision and scientific knowledge of disciplines like acoustics and chemistry. It's used to get a full-sensory picture of an area or target.**
>
> **Geospatial intelligence (GEOINT). Intelligence gathered about the physical layout of an area, used to create maps for purposes such as finding safe routes for soldiers or first responders.**

You may have noticed that many government buildings have giant concrete barriers in front of them. These barriers prevent dangerous scenarios, such as a truck bomber driving a vehicle filled with explosives into a building. Barriers, border patrols, airport security, fences, guards stationed in strategic locations—all of these are part of the mission of antiterrorist teams, that is, to prevent a terrorist from being able to physically carry out an attack by fixing vulnerabilities.

Many aspects of counterterrorism involve the more traditional picture of combating terrorist efforts seen in action movies—a specialized team, swooping into a country to track down a terrorist cell planning out an attack.

The FBI Fly Team is just one of those counterterrorism units. The Fly Team is comprised of FBI employees with special skills, who are prepared at a moment's notice to head to any location in the world to respond to an existing or imminent terrorist threat. One of the team's major roles is to figure out the situation: who is involved, who or what the likely targets are, and where an attack is about to happen.

The Fly Team's role is to set up the initial investigation, but there are many other units and many other activities that are involved in counterterrorism actions and investigations. Many of these groups are more like a collection of specialized units that, while performing their specific roles, work together to achieve a common goal. Some of the counterterrorism actions these units focus on include locating and defusing explosives, examining explosives to figure out who made them, figuring out how and where terrorists get their money, and intelligence gathering and analysis.

The Intelligence Community

Intelligence is central to both counterterrorism and antiterrorism activities. Since intelligence gathering is at the heart of AT/CT operations, many of the available jobs on an AT/CT force will be in intelligence analysis. Those people and organizations that work in intelligence refer to themselves as the intelligence community (IC).

A large version of the Central Intelligence Agency's seal greets those who pass through the lobby of CIA headquarters in Langley, Virginia. The seal has been around since 1950.

Intelligence is both the final result that comes out of gathering, analyzing, and explaining information about other countries or groups and the name for the process that leads to the final result.

Without intelligence, there would be very little information about terrorists and their activities. Any potential acts they would plan to commit and any potential groups or areas they would plan to target would largely be a mystery. Intelligence gives a task force its direction; it helps the task force know where it needs to direct its efforts, and it is what helps the group accomplish its mission from beginning to end.

The intelligence process is really a series of continuous cycles. As one is

The National Security Agency's Threat Operation's Center in Maryland is a twenty-four-hours-a-day operation where employees monitor intelligence and cyber threats and ensure that the United States' most confidential information is safe from cyber attacks.

completed, the information that it produced is used to begin the next. The initial phase is called the management phase. Before intelligence can be collected or analyzed, the first step is to figure out what needs to be collected. To do this, members of the IC called issue coordinators study previous intelligence and meet with government officials, the president, and representatives from government agencies to figure out their concerns and needs.

Once the IC knows where there is a need for intelligence, it can begin the collection process, known as data gathering. The name of the process describes exactly what happens— intelligence, in all its forms, is collected.

The pile of intelligence that is collected in the data gathering process is a mass of reports, photos, codes, and measurements. On its own, it means very little. The information needs to be organized and presented in a way that makes sense to those who will be analyzing it. This is the interpretation process.

The next stage is the analysis and reporting process. The data is reformatted during the interpretation process, but the analysis process gives that data meaning. People that interpret the data, known as analysts, are highly knowledgeable about the issues or regions that the data they are studying relates to. This knowledge helps analysts make sense of the data. Not all the data will be reliable. Not all of it will be useful. The analyst uses his or her expertise to determine what is important and try to predict a terrorist group's next move.

The analyst writes a report, sending it along to an official who will do a final review before sending it to the president, other officials, and members of the National Security Council. These officials will review the intelligence, act upon it if necessary, and, based on what they have received, ask for more intelligence. At that point, the intelligence cycle begins again.

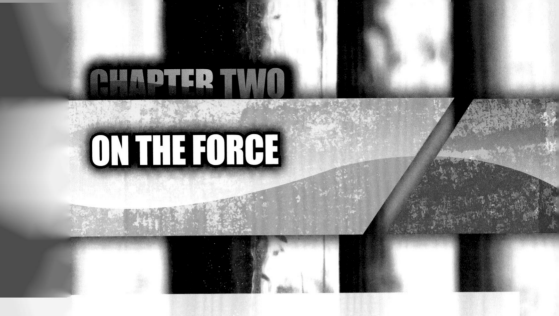

There are two definitions that apply to counterterrorism and antiterrorism task forces: 1) a group that exists to take on a specific task, and 2) a military group that exists to carry out a mission. Both types of AT/CT task forces exist: those that tackle issues like cyber-terrorism or work on ways to generally combat AT and CT; and military units that carry out actions, such as completing raids on terrorist hideouts.

Choose Your Task Force

While most of this section will examine three specific task forces in greater detail, the following list provides a general idea of some of the available options, grouped by governmental or geographic categories.

U.S. Armed Forces: Elite, highly trained groups, many of the task forces here are the ones that undergo operations to go after and capture terrorists and terrorist cells. This includes the U.S. Army's 1st Special Forces Operational Detachment-Delta, or Delta Force, and the Naval Special Warfare Development Group (DEVGRU). Most of the information surrounding these organizations and their missions is top secret.

Federal Government Organizations: Two major ones in this group are the Joint Terrorism Task Force (JTTF), explored in detail later in this section, and the Anti-Terrorism Advisory Council (ATAC). The role of the ATAC is to make sure information is shared through all levels of government, provide CT training, and organize terrorism investigations and the prosecution process for captured terrorists. For both these groups, there is at least one branch of the task force in each state. The members of these task forces represent dozens of different organizations that change depending on the specific needs of each state or region the task force represents.

State: Some states run their own CT and AT departments. An example is the Florida Regional Domestic Security Task Force, split into seven regions, and run by the sheriff's office and the police. The role of this group is to anticipate, protect against, and respond to potential terrorist attacks.

International Groups: The most globally expansive group in this category is the United Nations' (UN) CTITF, or the Counter-Terrorism Implementation Task Force, which overseas the UN's CT efforts. For those more interested in police work, there is INTERPOL's Fusion Task Force (FTF),

The 1st Battalion's Operational Detachment Alpha 3112 engages in an evacuation training exercise. This unit is part of the U.S. Army's Special Forces, known more familiarly as Green Berets.

comprised of members from more than 120 countries who come together to monitor, locate, gather, and share intelligence on terrorist organizations.

The JTTF

In 2009, the FBI received important information from New Scotland Yard, London's police force. During a terrorist investigation, New Scotland Yard had come across an e-mail about a man named Najibullah Zazi, who was living in Denver. When the Denver JTTF office received the tip, they began to monitor Zazi's activities. Denver JTTF members noted his purchase of hydrogen peroxide and acetone—common household items that also

THE NJTTF

Located near Washington, D.C., the National Joint Terrorism Task Force (NJTTF) is there to provide support to the JTTFs by coordinating their work, providing training, and answering intelligence-related questions from JTTF members.

Like the JTTF, the NJTTF is comprised of different members representing different government departments, military, and law enforcement agencies. Members must be invited to join and pass a top secret security clearance. Two officials run the NJTTF jointly, one from the FBI and one from the Department of Homeland Security (DHS).

A typical day of work for the NJTTF begins at 5:00 AM. At the office, members receive reports on new and important information. They spend the next few hours reading the reports in preparation for the 9:30 AM meeting, where the use of cell phones, computers, or other electronic equipment is banned. During the briefing, the news for that day is discussed, and all members update the team with new information from the agencies they represent. Members of the FBI's counterterrorism watch group are also there to provide the latest information on terrorist threats.

When the briefing is over, members of the NJTTF splinter off. Some report back information that is important for the agencies they're representing to know about. Some work on helping JTTF members complete investigations by answering questions, doing background checks on individuals, and finding ways to provide intelligence JTTF members are missing. This highlights the importance of having so many different member agencies participate in the NJTTF and JTTF; the databases and investigations of agencies outside the FBI may provide key information the FBI wouldn't otherwise be able to access.

When the NJTTF becomes aware of a threat that requires action, it will contact the regional JTTF office that will need to respond or all of the JTTFs if the scale of the threat is larger.

When there is an actual threat, the NJTTF's process is not changed, but members work more hours, and the speed of work accelerates. Members work through the week and weekend, until the threat is handled.

The **NJTTF** also runs special projects. These include:

Operation TRIPWIRE: This program is focused on information gathering and sharing, especially with regard to locating potential terrorist cells before they take action. The program requests information from different types of businesses, such as asking the airline industry for information on passengers who act strangely or finding out if hardware stores have had customers who purchased large quantities of potential bomb-making materials.

Correctional Intelligence Initiative: This program focuses on preventing prison inmates from radicalizing. Prisons are a popular place for jailed members of terrorist groups to get other inmates to join their movement.

Rail Liaison Intelligence Program: This program focuses on gathering information on terrorist plots related to train travel.

Military Working Group: This small group whose members represent the twelve Department of Defense agencies works on threats related to the military.

happen to be common ingredients in certain types of bombs. They watched as Zazi spent two nights in a hotel and proceeded to send FBI technicians over to the room after he checked out. They discovered evidence that Zazi had brought his purchases to the hotel and had boiled down the substances to make them more powerful.

On September 9, 2009, Zazi left Denver, driving east in a rented car. In need of information about where Zazi was headed, the Denver JTTF asked the Colorado State Police to pull him over. This wasn't hard to do, since Zazi was speeding, and the police used that as a pretense. The cops who pulled him over learned that Zazi was heading to New York. At that point, the JTTF didn't know whether Zazi was running away from an attack happening in Denver or planning one for New York. The Denver JTTF alerted FBI agents across the country, who tracked him as he made his way to New York. After being stopped a few times in New York, Zazi realized the stops were not coincidental and got rid of all his materials and evidence and flew back to Colorado.

Zazi was met by FBI agents, who questioned him for three days, got a search warrant for his apartment, and finally arrested him. In February 2010, Zazi pleaded guilty in court. What had Zazi been planning to do when he had driven to New York? Along with two friends, he was planning to carry out suicide bombings on three very busy subway lines in New York City.

FBI agents conduct a search of Najibullah Zazi's apartment in Aurora, Colorado, after Zazi's failed terrorist plot. Notice the different uniforms of those involved in the search, which draws on agents with diverse expertise.

If a terrorist in the United States has been captured or a plot thwarted, it is likely the JTTF has been involved. The JTTF is involved with most aspects of a terrorist investigation: gathering and sharing intelligence, conducting investigations, and arresting suspected terrorists.

According to the FBI's Facts and Figures 2010–11 report, there are over 100 JTTFs in all, with at least one in every state, with over 4,400 participating members. Each JTTF is led by an FBI Special Agent in Charge (SAC) with the exception of Washington, D.C.; New York; and Los Angeles, which are led by an Assistant Director in Charge, a higher-level position. Though run by the FBI, the JTTFs represent the collaborative efforts of over forty differ-ent agencies and organizations. In the ranks of JTTF membership you will find state and local police officers, border patrol agents, SWAT team members, language experts, intelligence analysts, representa-tives from the attorney's office, and finance and computer specialists, among others. To join a JTTF, a member must be invited or request to be invited and pass a security clearance.

SEAL Team Six

The Naval Special Warfare Development Group, or DEVGRU, is better known to the world as SEAL Team Six. Although the name SEAL Team Six is no longer officially in use, the name has stuck, and it is how the group is most commonly referred to. SEAL Team Six is used to carry out counterterrorism operations overseas, including capturing terrorists and rescuing hostages.

As the name suggests, the members of SEAL Team Six are Navy SEALs. SEAL stands for sea, air, land. To become a SEAL, candidates go through rigorous training that prepares them for secret operations using spe-cial strategies, tactics, and advanced technological equipment

The special patrol exertion/extraction technique—displayed here by a group of Navy SEALs at a Veteran's Day ceremony at the National Navy UDT-SEAL Museum— allows teams to enter and exit locations where helicopters can't land.

in any environment. For a SEAL, training never ends, and when units are assigned a specific mission, the unit may spend weeks planning and training to carry out that mission. SEAL Team Six is one of a number of SEAL units under the command of the Naval Special Warfare Group, which itself is part

This patch is worn by members of SEAL Team Six, or so it is believed. The unit's existence isn't officially acknowledged, but patches like this one, held by its owner, offer bits of physical evidence.

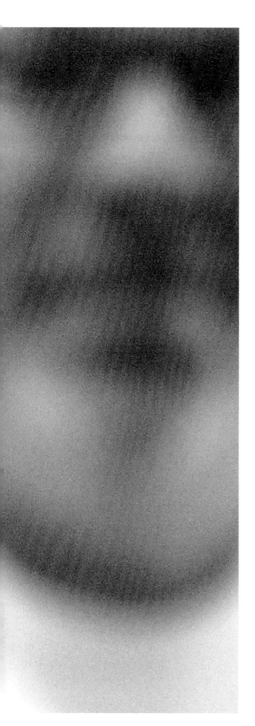

of the Joint Special Operations Command, the military unit responsible for the secret special operations units of the military.

Most of the information surrounding SEAL Team Six is classified, or kept secret by the government, and only a few of the group's missions are known to the general public. When a SEAL Team Six mission does make it into the newspaper, it is for one of two reasons: something went really wrong (usually the death of either a team member or a hostage) or something went really right—a notorious terrorist was taken out during a dramatic hostage rescue. This was the case when SEAL Team Six parachuted into Somalia one night in January 2012 to rescue two hostages who had been held by Somali pirates for three months.

The hostages, American Jessica Buchanan and Dane Poul Hagen Thisted, worked for a charity organization called the Danish Refugee Council. They were on their way to the airport after conducting a workshop in Somalia when two trucks filled with Somali pirates stopped them and took the two hostage.

In January, after the pirates had turned down a ransom offer of $1.5 million and there was word that Jessica Buchanan was in bad shape, the United States, with the approval of President Barack Obama, decided to take action. About twenty-four SEALs, mostly from SEAL Team Six, were flown into Somalia, where they parachuted into the country and then walked 2 miles (3.2 km) in the darkness to the location where the pirates were keeping the hostages.

There, the SEALs killed nine armed pirates who were also keeping explosives nearby. The two hostages were rescued, and the SEALs and hostages, all unharmed, flew out of the country.

CHAPTER THREE

THE MANY PATHS TO A TASK FORCE

For work on a CT or AT task force, a predetermined path to a task does not exist. There is no specific degree to earn in college, no specific graduate school that candidates need to attend, and no specific test to pass that makes someone a registered CT or AT expert.

In most cases, positions on a task force aren't even openings that a candidate can apply for by sending out a résumé and cover letter. Many of the people who work on a task force have been appointed, meaning that someone in a high position has recommended them to a task force. Often, the appointees have had years of job experience in an area vital to the needs of the task force, in addition to extensive training in CT- and AT-related issues.

While the requirements and steps to obtaining a position on a task force may be more uncertain and open-ended, that uncertainty provides for more opportunities. This applies to the types of courses someone interested in the field can study in college, or even, in some cases, whether someone wants to go to college

Student programs provide an opportunity to see the work of agencies up close. Here, students from the Stephen Tyrone Johns Summer Youth Leadership program visit the FBI Training Facility in Quantico, Virginia.

at all. This applies to the types of internships and special student programs available. While there is no single path to a task force, there are many ways to get to the goal.

A position on a task force may be the ultimate goal, but there are many decisions and steps to make along the way. One will be deciding on an area of focus or college major. Another will be exploring different job opportunities through internships. Another will be getting that first job. Once you get the job, working hard, taking on roles that relate to CT and AT work, and participating in available CT and AT training opportunities will all be crucial to getting recognized and scoring a recommendation for a position on a task force.

PROGRAMS: STARTING EARLY

While many internship opportunities and programs are geared toward college students, there are options for high school students as well. Below are a few.

Junior Reserve Officers' Training Corps (JROTC): A program for students interested in learning more about the military. The program allows students to explore the possibility of a career in the armed forces and gain basic military experience.

Customs and Border Protection Law Enforcement Explorer Program: Allows students fourteen and older the opportunity to work with customs and border protection (CBP) agents at airports and seaports, help with surveillance, and gain familiarity and experience with the work of CBP.

Study Abroad/Student Exchange: Your school may offer a student exchange program that allows you to live abroad for a term. If your school doesn't have a program, organizations such as the Rotary Club offer their own exchange programs.

Before undertaking all this preparation, study, and work, it is important to figure out how and where your own skills and interests fit in. The interests and skills that make someone a good candidate for work in the field are a varied mix of general and specific aptitudes. Some skills are necessary for working on any type of task force, while others are crucial to specialized task forces. The following explores those skills and interests.

Interest Inventory

You may or may not already have a strong interest in CT or AT, but the study of CT and AT is just one of the subject areas that can signify that this is the career for you. Often, you can combine an interest in CT and AT with an interest in another subject or hobby that can allow you to specialize, or focus, on a specific aspect of CT and AT work. Here are some examples.

Culture/history: An interest in the traditions and practices of different social and ethnic groups throughout the world, or knowledge about the history of other countries is crucial for intelligence analysts. It is by applying a deep understanding of a country and its people that raw intelligence is turned in to useful analysis. Knowing the customs and practices of a foreign city, country, or region also helps team members operate on the ground.

Technology/computer science: Do you like to code Web sites and apps? Are you the first one of your friends to discover and master the latest programs, apps, and gadgets? Many terrorist organizations maintain an online presence, with members who communicate with each other online and use the Internet to recruit new members. People who specialize in cyber-counterterrorism work to locate, decode, and dismantle those networks. Knowledge of coding is also needed to create programs to monitor online conversations and information exchanges.

Science: There are many ways in which task forces need members with deep scientific knowledge, from conducting forensic investigations to figuring out how to identify and reduce the threat of explosives and IEDs to assessing chemical

Preparation and training are integral to protecting the country. Members of DHS's National Cybersecurity & Communications Integration Center get ready for Cyber Storm III, a real-time exercise to practice warding off cyber attacks.

biological, and nuclear threats.

Finance: Those who enjoy dealing with the comings and goings of money can find a place for themselves on a task force following the money trail that can lead investigators to discover a terrorist cell.

Skill Inventory

The following skills are more generalized skills that task forces will be looking for to make sure job candidates are a good fit for the team and prepared for the emotional and psychological aspects of the job.

Analytical: As the name implies, analysts rely on analytical thinking to process information, look out for things that don't make sense or contradict each other, and apply knowledge

Collaboration is a key aspect of CT and AT work. Here, cooperation is on the global level as the U.S. Marine Corps Fleet Antiterrorism Security Team Pacific participates in a joint exercise in South Korea.

they already have to new information they receive. It requires someone to take different bits of information and form them into a logical whole to figure out the answer. Analysts aren't the only members of task forces who use analytical skills— the nature of the work requires teams to constantly apply analytical skills to shifting scenarios that affect planning and action.

Interpersonal skills: Put in familiar terms, having good interpersonal skills means knowing how to deal with or communicate well with people. Task force work is teamwork. Being able to work successfully on a team and to get along with team members, and to know how to listen and when to contribute—all these abilities are necessary for a team to be able to carry out its mission successfully. Sharing intelligence is a back-and-forth, trust-based process where being able to create and cultivate contacts and relationships with other agencies is necessary; having strong interpersonal skills gets this job done.

Oral and written communication: Oral and written communication skills require the ability to deliver information clearly and in a way that makes sense. For writing, this means having a good grasp of grammar, syntax, and sentence and paragraph structure. It also means being able to deliver complex, important information succinctly. For both writing and speaking, this also means knowing your audience. In CT and AT, different groups and agencies use different vocabularies based on their areas of expertise. When sharing information—a constant, important part of task force work—the message needs to be tailored in such a way that all groups involved have the same understanding of a situation.

Mental toughness: This is the ability of someone to push him- or herself to keep going, bounce back from failure, and deal with pressure. For the task forces that operate in the field on covert, dangerous missions, gaining entry onto such a team requires passing a grueling physical test. The test may last weeks, and candidates will perform difficult tasks on little sleep. The tests are designed to make people want to quit. Evaluators are looking to see whether the candidates are able to perform and make the right decisions while under stress and can push themselves to go on when they are ready to give up. Operations in the field are unpredictable, and merely being strong is not good enough. Task force members need to display good judgment and the ability to act quickly, calmly, and decisively in chaotic conditions.

Make Yourself Competitive Now

The competition for careers on AT and CT task forces is intense, with lots of impressive résumés from skilled candidates who have advanced degrees and hours and hours of CT and AT training. There are things you can work on now that will help make you stand out years from now.

Consider the story of George Piro. The FBI was involved in the second Iraq war from the early days, often working jointly

The New York City Police Academy is the starting point for those looking to join the New York Police Department. Here, a recruit receives weapons training.

The Many Paths to a Task Force | **53**

with the military. One of the roughly sixteen FBI agents working in the country was a member of the FBI's Fly Team, George Piro. Piro had a major advantage that would make him an important part of U.S. operations in Baghdad: Piro was a native Arabic speaker. Native Arabic speakers were in high demand, and Piro ended up accompanying army officials on many missions, including going undercover as an Iraqi to follow and attempt to trap a bomber. Piro had been an FBI agent for just five years when he got the biggest role of his career. Following the capture of Saddam Hussein, Iraq's deposed dictator, Piro became Hussein's major interrogator. Day after day, Piro would speak with the former dictator for hours, learning how Hussein had managed to stay hidden from the U.S. forces looking for him and discovering that most of the WMD the United States was looking for hadn't existed since the 1990s.

To get to that role, Piro had gone from the air force to the police academy. While serving as an officer, Piro went to night school to get the bachelor's degree that would allow him to be eligible to apply to the FBI. While Piro put a lot of work into becoming a Special Agent, his knowledge of Arabic allowed him to have the unique, historical role he did.

Not everyone can be a native speaker of a foreign language, but learning and mastering a new language is a different story. Since it's generally easier for young people to learn languages, starting as soon as possible is advantageous. Many job openings for CT and AT work will place candidates who speak certain in-demand languages higher in the candidate pool. Some of those languages are Arabic, Chinese, Farsi, Hebrew, Hindi, Japanese, Korean, Pashtu, Punjabi, Russian, Spanish, Turkish, Urdu, and Vietnamese.

Related to but separate from foreign language experience is foreign travel experience, especially extended experience abroad, such as through a volunteer or exchange program. Having experience abroad demonstrates comfort with working abroad, which is important since travel may be part of the job. Foreign experience also helps with understanding other cultures, which is important for analytical and investigative work.

As cyber-terrorism becomes an increasingly important part of terrorist activity, the demand for people who use advanced computer skills to fight terrorism will likely also rise. Learning computer programming is a useful activity to take up. There are even books and online programs that target their lessons to teenagers.

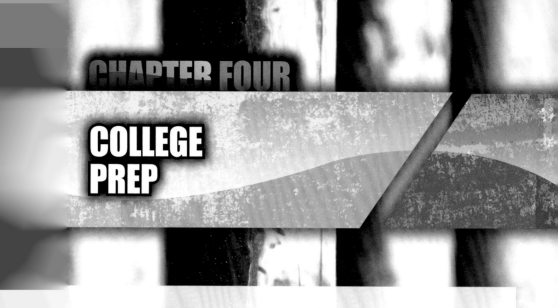

CHAPTER FOUR

COLLEGE PREP

Most jobs in the fields of CT and AT, and by extension, on a CT or AT task force, will require at least a bachelor's degree, or the degree you get when you graduate from a four-year college. You must choose a college major, or subject focus, for your degree. The following are some of the more common options.

Choosing Your Major

International relations (IR): This may also be known as international affairs or regional studies (for example, Middle Eastern studies). This degree focuses on the cultural, political, and economic systems of different countries and regions. Student may also study global issues (such as CT, ethnic conflict, global health, or poverty), regional and international organizations, and political and international relations theory. The specifics of this degree will vary depending on the school. There are usually opportunities to specialize within the major, and some schools offer a terrorism or security studies focus.

In terms of careers in AT and CT, the IR degree is almost like a universal entry ticket for those looking to get into the field. This isn't to say that this degree will guarantee a job in the field, but the degree does demonstrate some very attractive qualities to employers: a culturally sensitive (one presumes) candidate with a knowledge about the people and countries CT and AT teams work with and within.

Language/linguistics: Choosing this major will allow you to master a foreign language and also learn something about the cultures and regions that claim that language as their mother tongue. Since a lot of intelligence collected overseas is in a foreign language, the intelligence needs to be translated and given proper context. This is the job of the linguist. Having advanced foreign language skills can also lead to a role in the field, as was the case with Agent Piro's work in Iraq.

Science/engineering: A degree in chemistry, biochemistry, or engineering can lead to a role in a forensic science unit specializing in preventing and investigating CBRN attacks by terrorist organizations, a position in the Joint Improvised Explosive Device Defeat Organization (JIEDDO), or work as a bomb technician. Members of these teams work in cooperation with task forces to prevent or respond to terrorist attacks.

Computer science: Computer science majors, who study computer systems and related topics like programming,

High demand for foreign language skills is exemplified by this Arabic class for Marines at Camp Pendleton. The class is part of the Center for Advanced Operational Cultural Learning, created about six years ago.

algorithms, and cryptography, can find work on cyber-counterterrorism units locating chat rooms and forums for terrorist organizations and creating programs that will help law enforcement officials track terrorists online.

Finance: A degree in accounting, finance, or business could lead to a position on a task force that uses banking information to discover terrorist operations and cells. The United States, for example, sends members of the Departments of Treasury, State, and Justice to participate in the Financial Action Task Force (FATF), a group comprised of over thirty member countries that work together to find terrorists by tracking money that gets to and comes from terrorists.

Law: A law degree, or Juris Doctor degree, can lead to a career in the U.S Department of Justice, whose state and regional attorneys general are in charge of their state's or region's ATAC.

Alternatives to College

If you don't believe college is right for you, aren't yet ready for college, or are looking for a nontraditional type of college experience, there are a few available alternatives. Most of these, however, will require additional on-the-job training and certifications to position you for a task force.

Law enforcement will provide one of the major opportunities, as it is the local, state, and federal law enforcement officials who make up the bulk of the JTTFs, in addition to FBI

BUD/S

Becoming a member of one of the armed services' premier counterterrorism forces, the Navy SEALs, requires passing an extremely long and strenuous series of training and tests that lasts over two years. During your training, you put your body and mind through arduous challenges like dropping from helicopters without a parachute, diving deep under the ocean with your weapon prepped, scaling multistory walls, and dragging tires strapped to your body with a chain through the sand.

It begins with **SEAL Prep School**, a screening for prospective candidates that tests their readiness for the next level of training, called basic underwater demolition/SEAL (BUD/S). BUD/S training lasts six months and is split into different sections. Candidates spend the first three weeks in orientation, which prepares candidates for what's ahead: three weeks of timed 4-mile (6.4 km) runs in boots, obstacle courses, and 2-mile (3.2 km) swims with time requirements that keep getting shorter. The following week is one of the toughest in a candidate's training: five and a half days of continuous physical activity, done on four hours of sleep—not per night, but total.

If candidates pass that phase, proving their mental and physical strength, they continue on with training, learning long distance combat diving, parachute and free fall jumping, rappelling, cold weather survival, and weapons and explosives training, among other skills. Candidates put all the skills they've learned to use for three weeks on San Clemente Island in California. If candidates pass those training units—seventeen weeks plus the twenty-six-week-long SEAL qualification training, they graduate, and can be called SEALs.

Don't think the training is over. Newly minted SEALs get assigned to a unit, and spend eighteen more months in training with their unit and as individuals training in a specialty. All this will make you prepared to jump, swim, fly, or hike into enemy territory to complete your mission.

Cadets who attend the United States Military Academy at West Point have the opportunity to study terrorism in-depth, such as the students here attending an Advanced Terrorism Studies class.

agents. Each law enforcement agency will have its own hiring practices and requirements for JTTF participation, so you will need to research the law enforcement agency you're interested in to learn about the application requirements. Many of the federal law enforcement opportunities will be in departments within the DHS, such as becoming a border patrol agent with U.S. Customs and Border Protection.

Another option is to go into military service, which has opportunities for those with and without college degrees. Some military units dealing with counterterrorism, especially dealing with intelligence, require bachelor's degrees. There is also the option to combine military experience with a bachelor's degree by gaining acceptance to a service academy, such as the United States Military Academy, more commonly known as West Point. There, students can, if they choose, focus on counterterrorism studies. Upon graduation, students enter the army as officers and must commit to staying in the army for five years. There is a service academy for every branch of the military.

Those who join the military without a bachelor's degree will take the Armed Services Vocational Aptitude Battery (ASVAB). The ASVAB tests the skills and abilities of recruits to see which types of careers and programs within the military they are suited for. You can take this test before enlisting to see if the programs you're suited for match your interests.

Internships

The good news about exploring career opportunities in CT and AT, and figuring out if this type of career and lifestyle is for you, is that there are many internship opportunities available for college students. The following opportunities are some of the more prominent organizational internships, but be sure to check with your local law enforcement agencies to see if there are available opportunities closer to home. The internships here are for government agencies, which may undergo changes from time to time, so be sure to check each organization's Web site for the latest information.

CIA Undergraduate Internship Program — Analysis: Students accepted to this program spend either two full summers or one college semester and one summer working in Washington, D.C. The application process is intense and includes a medical, psychological, and background examination, a polygraph

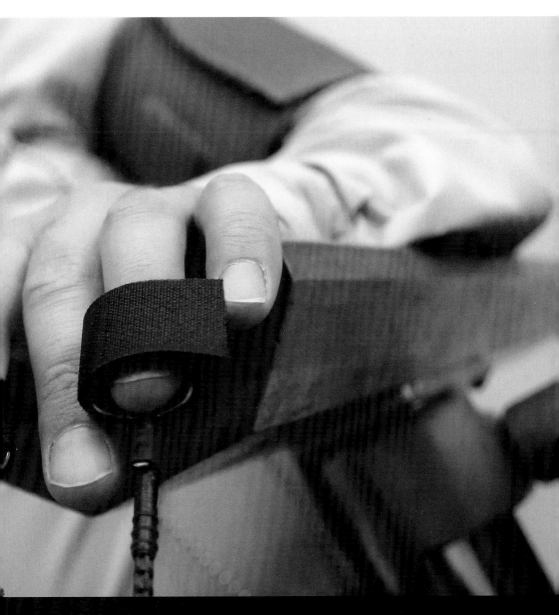

Polygraph interviews are required for many jobs with security clearances. The polygraph, or lie-detector machine, works by monitoring fluctuations of vital signs like your heartbeat, which change when you lie.

(lie detector) test, and an online application that requires you to discuss your background, educational history, skills, work experience, and foreign language proficiency, among other things. If you get in, you will be rewarded for your troubles with a paid internship in which you will do real analytical work, doing research and writing briefs on different issues and topics, as well as working on special projects and sitting in on meetings. Do a good job, and your reward just may be a full-time position as a CIA analyst after you graduate from college.

There are three basic eligibility requirements for the internship: you must be a U.S. citizen, a full-time student who has completed at least one year of college, and your GPA must be a 3.0 at minimum.

Since this is an extremely competitive internship, merely meeting the minimum requirement won't cut it. Foreign language proficiency, overseas travel, and military experience will all help make you a more competitive candidate. If you have an interest in a particular region of the world, build up your knowledge of the area and its people, customs, and culture, and be prepared to demonstrate your knowledge.

One final thing to keep in mind—the process takes an entire year, so be sure to plan ahead.

FBI Volunteer Internship Program: The "volunteer" in the title of this program indicates that it isn't a paid internship, but, like the CIA internship, it is still competitive and could lead to a permanent job after graduation. The requirements are also similar, including having a minimum 3.0 GPA and being a U.S. citizen. The internship is open to college juniors and seniors as well as graduate students and requires a background examination, interviews, and a polygraph in addition to the application. Students who are accepted will work with FBI employees for ten weeks in the summer and have a chance to learn more about the different types of FBI careers. Foreign language and travel abroad experience will get you ahead. Candidates with specific majors may be expressly sought out—computer/tech majors, such as computer science, IT, and computer/software engineering, are currently in high demand.

Special Programs and Scholarships

In addition to internships, many organizations offer special programs that provide students training, scholarships, and/or internships in exchange for a pledge to commit to a certain amount of years to working in a government agency. Keep in mind that these aren't necessarily specific to CT or AT but provide candidates with the experience and contacts that may prove useful as they try to join a task force.

Pat Roberts Intelligence Scholars Program (PRISP): To be eligible for this program, candidates must have already completed an internship with an office that is part of the intelligence community. The program provides participants with a stipend while in college, and participants agree to serve as full-time employees in an intelligence office for a

BLINDSIDED BY BAD HABITS

As a member of a task force, you are entrusted with knowing and keeping the country's most sensitive secrets. With every job in a task force, and most jobs that get you to a task force, getting the job will depend on two questions. The first, like any job you apply to, is, are you the right candidate for the job? In the world of **AT** and **CT**, however, being qualified is not enough. The second question is, can you be trusted? No matter how qualified you are, if you can't be trusted, you can forget about a career in this field.

The decision about whether you are a trustworthy candidate isn't based on a gut feeling by your employer but hinges on your getting a top secret security clearance. The security clearance involves a questionnaire you fill out that has you provide a detailed account of your activities, including schooling, work, places you have lived, places you have travelled, and mental and emotional health history. Investigators will conduct an interview with you and conduct checks on your friends, relatives, and employers.

For most organizations, passing the security clearance isn't the only test of personal integrity. Many agencies explicitly list additional deal breakers. For those serious about careers in the field, be warned, in many cases youthful indiscretions or inappropriate behaviors can end your career before it's begun.

Illegal drug use is a big disqualifier, and many agencies, including the CIA and FBI, will ask you about your history. Using any illegal drugs other than marijuana or prescription pills even once will close down your application. There is a very slight tolerance of past use of marijuana or illegally used prescription drugs, but it had to have been used sparingly and several years before you apply for an internship or job.

Bad credit, and more specifically defaulting on, or not being able to pay, student loans is often another disqualifier. Some organizations will even frown on overdue library books. Be careful how you use your credit cards and pay your bills—living beyond your means or being heavily in debt could demonstrate that you could be bribed by a country or organization willing to trade money for secrets.

(continued on page 70)

One final thing to watch out for is what and how you share. The picture you present of yourself online and on your social networks will be examined. Be careful about what you post and be conscious of the image you are projecting, because that image will give your background investigators clues about whether you are trustworthy, are discrete, and show good judgment—all qualities required for your background check.

minimum of eighteen months following graduation. The program looks for candidates who have expertise in a particular region of the world, language proficiency—especially in an Asian, Central Asian, or Middle Eastern language—and educational experience or coursework in international relations, science, engineering, computer science, national security, and finance, among other subjects.

Recent Graduates Program: Part of the government's Pathways Program, this allows recent graduates to apply to a government agency for one year of work and training, with the chance of becoming full-time employees at the end of the program. Applicants must look for available openings with the agency of their choice.

Presidential Management Fellows: The Presidential Management Fellows Program allows participants with a recent graduate degree to spend two years working with a

The FBI trains not only new recruits and employees but citizens from the Quantico area as well. Participants invited to FBI Citizens' Academy undergo a two-month training similar to the one that new agents receive.

government agency, learn about the work of the agency, design and complete a special project, and receive hours of job and skills training. The program does not guarantee a position; candidates who are selected to be finalists attend a special job fair where they meet and interview with participating government agencies, including branches of the military, for open positions.

Boren Scholarships: Undergraduate students who complete the intensive application process and are accepted spend either a semester or a year living in and studying the language and culture of a foreign country identified as important to U.S. security needs. After graduating from college, candidates agree to spend a year working with an agency dealing with national security or intelligence.

Critical Language Scholarship Program: This fully funded program is open to undergraduates who have completed at least one year of college. The program provides students interested in learning or improving skills in a specific foreign language with the chance to spend eight weeks of the summer abroad, immersed in intensive language study. Participants also take trips and learn about the culture of the region by spending significant time with native residents.

In addition to these options, the college you attend will likely have study abroad programs. Some may also have a semester in Washington program, in which you can spend a semester living and interning in Washington, D.C.

CHAPTER FIVE

GETTING THE JOB

As a newly minted college graduate, or soon to be college graduate, you decide that a career on a CT or AT task force is what you want. You begin a job search but know you can't simply check the Internet and different organizations for entry positions on an AT or CT task force. You know this because those entry positions don't really exist. It takes years to build up enough experience and training to be appointed to or try out for a position. Your focus then, as a fresh-faced holder of a bachelor's degree, is to build up that experience.

The most practical strategy is to apply to work for an organization that works on CT or AT issues, has a CT department, or is a member of an AT/CT task force.

The type of job you look for will depend on your interests and the degree you have, but if it's a government job you're trying to get, any organization you're interested in will direct you to start your search in the same place. USAjobs.gov is

As the cap on this graduate underscores, the job market is tight and competitive. This makes it even more crucial to take advantage of the programs and classes available that will help you stand out.

the site where all federal jobs are posted and where you apply to those jobs.

Another option, if you had been considering gaining military experience, is to apply to join the military as an officer. This will require attending the officer candidate school of the specific branch you're applying for and agreeing to serve as an officer for a specific amount of time.

G-Men

If joining the FBI is your goal, there are two ways to accomplish this. You can either apply to become part of the professional staff, or you can apply to become an FBI agent. The application process for joining the professional staff is the same as applying to the other agencies;

SEARCH OPTIONS

The list of departments that deal with intelligence and **CT** and **AT** is long. Here are some of the places for you to consider.

Department of Homeland Security (DHS): The **DHS** was created following the **9/11** attacks. The **DHS** has an office of intelligence and analysis, as well as numerous agencies that do **AT** and **CT** work, such as **U.S. Immigration and Customs Enforcement (ICE)**, **U.S. Customs and Border Protection (CBP)**, and the **Federal Emergency Management Agency (FEMA)**.

Department of Defense: The **DOD** has numerous agencies involved in security, including the **National Security Agency (NSA)**, which deals in all types of cryptology, or code breaking, and computer and math analysis. As well, each military branch has its own office of intelligence, with some of those jobs available to civilians.

Department of Energy (DOE): This one may seem surprising, but the **DOE** has an intelligence office that focuses on nuclear weapons and technology.

Department of Treasury (DOT): For the economics and finance majors out there, the **DOT** has its own intelligence office.

> *Environmental Protection Agency (EPA):*
> **Another seemingly unusual option, the EPA has
> hazardous materials (hazmat) units that assist
> the FBI in responding to incidents involving
> WMD or biological and chemical warfare.**

you will have to search for and apply to available positions on
the USAjobs.gov Web site.

To be eligible to apply for a Special Agent position, you
must be a U.S. citizen and at least twenty-three years old
and younger than thirty-six when you start. You must have a
four-year college or university degree, three years of professional work experience, and a driver's license.

The process begins with an online application, available
each year for a short window of time. Selected applicants are
chosen to move on to phase I testing, which involves taking a
series of written tests on logical thinking, judgment, and your
work style. You'll need to pass phase I to move on to phase II,
but that might not be enough. Phase II candidates are chosen
based on the types of skills and experience the FBI needs out
of its agents at a given point in time, so passing phase I
represents a chance, but not a guarantee, to move on to
phase II. Don't think you've left testing behind in phase I.
Phase II involves a written test and an interview with three
FBI agents consisting of thirteen questions. If you pass phase
II, you may receive a conditional letter of employment. This
means you can become an FBI agent...if you pass a few more

The intelligence community engages in many outreach efforts to fill its foreign language needs. At the IC Heritage Summit, shown here, native speakers from immigrant communities are encouraged to apply for intelligence jobs.

tests. For your employment to be official rather than conditional, there are a few final tests to pass: a physical exam that includes a 1.5 mile (2.4 km) run, a sprint, sit-ups and push-ups, a medical exam, a background exam, and a polygraph (lie detector) interview. If you pass, you're ready to begin your training at the FBI academy.

The Agency

The agency is a nickname for the CIA, and for those looking to make it into a task force as an analyst, it is one of the best places to develop in that role. CIA analysts read, interpret, and analyze some of the most important and sensitive information in the

NEW AGENT

Life as an **FBI** agent begins with a twenty-week new agent training course at the **FBI National Academy** in Quantico, Virginia. Training prepares new agents for every aspect of their careers. New agents undergo coursework and training in four areas: academics, case exercises, firearms training, and operational skills. Operational skills in a different career may involve banalities like forms and paperwork, but at the academy, new agents learn skills and techniques like trailing people, boxing, handcuffing and holding suspects, and learning how to work with witnesses and informants. The academic coursework prepares agents to be familiar with all the subjects, such as law and behavioral science, an **FBI** agent needs to know, as well as more experiential subjects such as interviewing techniques and intelligence gathering.

All of the training becomes a 3-D, surround-sound experience in Hogan's Alley, created with the help of the same people who create sets for movies. Hogan's Alley is the new agents' training playground, complete with the actors, homes, and businesses necessary to give the

FBI agents a real-life experience as they shoot, question, investigate, and arrest their way through the town in different simulations designed to feel as real as possible.

Once the new agents complete and pass their coursework, they are placed into one of five career paths—one of which is the counterterrorism division—and into one of the FBI's field offices. Agents can state their preference for both career path and field office, but this is no guarantee. With the career path preference an agent's background, education, and work experience come into play, so having a background that reflects interest and experience in CT will help here.

country, providing many break-in-the-case moments for terrorism investigations.

CIA counterterrorism analysts accomplish this through a 360-degree study and assessment of terrorist organizations, the structure of those organizations, their methods and targets, membership, and the reasons behind their actions.

To become an analyst, you need either a bachelor's or master's degree in international relations, security studies, or a similar subject. There is a preference for candidates who have studied a specific region, especially the Middle East or Southeast Asia, and bonus points, figuratively speaking, for those who have travel, study, or work abroad experience or can speak one of the critical foreign languages. Candidates also need a minimum 3.0 GPA. As in most cases with minimum requirements, the more you exceed the minimum requirements, the better the chance your application will be noticed.

Some college students may come face to face with agency reps on their own campus. Here, the CIA works to recruit students at a job fair at the University of Michigan.

In addition to these requirements, the position also requires the general skills that come up time and again in the CT and AT industry, namely, the ability to work as part of a team, to be good at problem solving, to possess strong communication skills, and handle the pressure of deadlines. Since being an analyst requires a lot of report writing or delivering, well-developed writing and speaking skills, including the ability to effectively get to the point, are a must.

The analyst application is completed online on the CIA's Web site and involves a cover letter, a detailed explanation of your experience, background, and qualifications, a five-to-eight page writing sample on your area of expertise, medical and psychological exams, a polygraph interview, and a background check.

For those candidates chosen to become CIA analysts, their careers begin at the Sherman Kent School for Intelligence Analysis. Part of CIA University, a training program that offers lessons and programs for CIA employees at all stages of their

Studying recruitment patterns may hold clues about the type of employees or particular skills agencies are in need of. A full-page CIA recruitment ad in an Arabic-language newspaper demonstrates the need for Arabic speakers.

career, new employees go through the career analyst program, or CAP. This is where employees learn how to deal effectively with intelligence, including lessons in how to think and write like an analyst, how to know when someone is lying or hiding things, and how to identify security threats.

CHAPTER SIX

GETTING AHEAD

All the work, effort, and arduous steps and tests you will need to pass through in order to get the job you want does not mean that, once you get that job, you will be able to coast through the rest of your career. Counterterrorism and antiterrorism are constantly evolving fields that change with new technologies, new trends in terrorism, and new directives from the federal government. Continuing education will be the story of your career. If you have a bachelor's degree, you will probably want to get your master's degree or at least begin taking classes that can lead you there. Many of the organizations you'll be working for will offer their own classes and special skills training in courses as diverse as foreign language training, computer programming, firearms, and explosives. Many of the specialized training courses you will take in the military will also count as credits toward a degree. Take advantage of every opportunity available to you.

There are many master's degree programs available in international relations, including those that focus on security studies, disaster management, and weapons of mass destruction. The school you choose to complete your master's degree will depend on a number of factors, and many of your

Many degree programs in terrorism studies offer real-world experience in addition to academic study. A Fairmont State University student searching for suspicious activity on social media sites will report discoveries to the CIA and FBI.

ll be influenced by your initial work experiences—
sts you want to explore in further detail and the
area of expertise you want to focus on. You may
choose overall top-tier programs like Johns
Hopkins Paul H. Nitze School of Advanced
International Studies, or the International
Security Policy Program at Columbia's School of
International and Public Affairs. You may choose
a program from one of the D.C.-area schools,
like Georgetown, George Washington University,
or American University, to take advantage of the
opportunities available in the nation's capital. In
your first few years on the job, you will have an
idea of what your needs are in this category.

Criticism, Assessments, and the Difficulties of the Job

Compare a photograph of FBI director Robert
Mueller from the time he was appointed head
of the FBI in 2001 to a photo taken less than
a decade later. What you will see is the face of a
man who has been aged by the stresses and
demands of holding one of the highest counterterrorism positions in this country. Where his
hair was brown, it is now gray. The previously
smooth face now bears a highway of wrinkles.

FBI director Robert Mueller speaks to Congress on threats to national security. His face shows the effects of over a decade serving as the head of the FBI.

It is the kind of aging that usually takes much longer. This photo represents a visual, outward sign of the pressures of this line of work.

Not everyone will age rapidly, but most everyone will experience the stress of the job. Analysts are confronted with boundless mountains of intelligence they sift through, hoping to spot, identify, and connect the pieces that will thwart terrorist activity that is underway or prevent a plan from ever coming to fruition—hoping they won't miss anything that can let a terrorist enter through the border unnoticed or plant a bomb. Members of task forces like SEAL Team Six and the Rangers go through round after round of prepping for action and then completing their tasks, entering territories and hideouts under enemy control. Task force leaders and CT officials encounter many nights of sleep broken up by middle of the night phone calls of seemingly dire and crucial tips. They aren't always, but they keep coming, and each one, however much of a dead end it might turn out to be, brings with it an adrenaline-addled call for planning and action. The career span of those working in CT and AT can be short. Burnout is common.

There are also external criticisms of how the government's CT and AT machine operates. According to the *Washington Post*, which ran an investigative project into how the country runs its national security program called "Top Secret America," the amount of organizations and offices engaged in CT and AT work is too large, with a lot of overlapping roles and efforts that ultimately hinder effective CT work.

THE HRT

One job that comes at the intersection of years of experience on the job, law enforcement or military experience, and tactical training (for example, training in situations involving firearms, weapons, and locating and going after suspects) is the FBI's Hostage Rescue Team (HRT). The HRT is the FBI unit devoted to combating terrorism through tactical methods. It is the HRT that is sent when local law enforcement and SWAT teams find a job too difficult or sensitive or when the situation requires the special expertise of the HRT, which includes the ability to climb down quickly from a rope attached to a helicopter in the middle of the air, dive in special scuba gear that doesn't create bubbles, and get quickly and quietly onto ships and into buildings.

To become a member of the HRT, you have to have already completed the long, complicated odyssey of becoming an FBI Special Agent and need to have been working as a Special Agent for at least three years. There is an alternate path, known at the Tactical Recruitment Program (TRP) for those with military or law enforcement experience. This is an option that allows candidates to apply for the HRT at the same time they apply to be Special Agents. However, the candidates need to be accepted to both programs and need to put in two years as Special Agents before they can be considered for an HRT position. On top of that, general military and law enforcement experience won't do: preference is given to law enforcement officials who have years of full-time tactical experience and members of the military whose experience comes from combat units or special forces like the Navy SEALs or Army Rangers.

The final requirement is passing the HRT test, where, while undergoing a series of physically taxing exercises on very little sleep, you try to avoid the exact thing the test is designed to make you do: breaking down from the unending physical and mental stress.

If you get on the team, you commit to spending your next four years there. The first eight months are spent on the highly specialized training you need as an HRT member. The rest are spent cycling through periods of training and operations. Although members of the HRT exercise and train every work day on tactics like firearms, sniper, and close quarter combat or fighting with the enemy in close distances, during the training cycle, the training goes deeper,

and HRT members undergo training and exercises that prepare them for different types of missions. HRT members get plenty of very realistic practice in a "shooting house" and on boats where the conditions mimic the very dangerous real-life scenarios that members may encounter.

Those same criticisms apply to intelligence gathering, where some believe that the amount of intelligence that is gathered and the never-ending daily analysis and report creation is too much for anyone to keep up with, possibly causing the important intelligence to get obscured.

Training, Training, and More Training

The more experience you gain early in your career, combined with the educational opportunities you take advantage of, the more opportunities will open up to you.

Fortunately, there are many training opportunities available for those in the field and aspiring to be in the field. In some cases, organizations will offer their own training, such as the CIA University, which in addition to its training course for entry-level analysts offers courses for professionals in different stages of their career. Military schools like the National War College offer officials, both in the armed forces and in government offices, advanced coursework and training in national security.

There are also many CT and AT training courses for law enforcement officials, which help candidates make the transition from law enforcement into CT and AT work and can make their résumés stand out as candidates for task forces. The Nationwide Suspicious Activity Reporting Initiative (NSI) offers law enforcement officials training in suspicious activity reporting (SAR). There are even classes specially designed for line officers, that is, those officers who are on patrol. The SAR classes provide AT training that allows law enforcement officials to look for signs and identify suspicious behavior hidden behind the seemingly benign scenes they encounter every day.

The Department of Homeland Security runs a training center offered to law enforcement at all levels, from local and tribal to international, called the Federal Law Enforcement Training Center (FLETC). There, law enforcement officials can take advantage of the many basic and advanced CT and AT courses offered, among them cyber-terrorism training, land transport antiterrorism, weapons of mass destruction, and hazardous materials.

The DHS also offers a specialized training school for officials and first responders—the police, firemen, and medical professionals who are the first on the scene of an attack—dealing with weapons of mass destruction. Called the Center for Domestic Preparedness, the school offers trainees classes and situational training for every aspect of a WMD or CBRNE incident. Some of the training students receive includes learning how to identify and handle hazardous materials, effective crowd control, handling a suicide bomb attack that is about to happen, and how to deal with the aftermath of a CBRNE attack.

The Future

Because so much of the work done in counterterrorism and antiterrorism is top secret, forecasting job prospects for the field isn't simply a matter of looking up statistics. In many cases, those statistics won't be available or even official, because of their top secret classification.

Even when there are numbers, the story the numbers tell is complicated. The HRT for example, has had less than three hundred members in total over its thirty-year history. The reason the numbers are so low has a lot to do with how hard it is to pass the test. Many try, but most drop out. There is a need for more HRT

Students attend a class at the Federal Law Enforcement Training Center (FLETC). On the floor are two park rangers learning how to arrest someone who is fighting back.

members, but the standards will not be lowered to accommodate that need. This is the case for a lot of special forces, so the chances of getting a job on one of those teams has more to do with the mental and physical toughness of candidates than with the availability of slots.

Members of an FBI SWAT team respond to a hostage situation at a bank in California. A man with a gun is holding a bank employee, and no one yet knows what the gunman wants.

Generally speaking, the field of CT and AT and many of the task forces in the area have grown immensely since September 11, 2001, and continue to grow, although at different rates. According to the Bureau of Labor Statistics, the job prospects for military careers are high and will be growing for years to come. Careers in law enforcement are also growing, but at a slower than average rate compared to all jobs, which indicates there will be increased competition in that field. Across the board, competition for jobs is high, so it is extremely important to gain as much skill, experience, and knowledge as possible early on. Paying attention to patterns in specific skills requested in job postings is also important—they hint at the future direction of the work. Currently, the emphasis on computer science demonstrates that the focus on cyber-terrorism is growing. The need for candidates fluent in critical languages is also ongoing. If you have an interest in those areas, developing them will give you an edge. No matter what type of CT or AT task force you are interested in, however, you will need to make yourself the candidate to beat.

advantageous Beneficial, or helpful for achieving a goal.

benign In medical terminology, something that is not harmful.

collaborative Describing an effort that involves teamwork.

dire Urgent or terrible.

disqualifier A condition, attribute, or situation that results in ineligibility.

experiential Relating to or coming as a result of experience.

hazardous materials Materials that are a public danger, such as explosive, toxic, or radioactive substances.

indiscretion An action that is indiscreet or showing bad judgment.

obscured Hidden or not easily visible.

prospective Relating to the future or something that is likely to happen.

radicalizing Causing to become extreme, especially as in political beliefs.

rigorous Very severe or harsh.

simulation An enactment or imitation designed to copy the real thing.

surveillance The act of watching a person or group very closely.

syntax The rules behind the order and structure of sentences.

tactical Relating to the use of weapons, troops, and vehicles in war or combat.

thwart To prevent a plan or act from occurring.

Canadian Security Intelligence Service (CSIS)
1941 Ogilvie Road
Ottawa ON K1J 1B7
Canada
(613) 993-9620
Web site: http://www.csis-scrs.gc.ca
The CSIS, Canada's intelligence organization, provides
background, reports, and papers on terrorism and
security issues.

Communications Security Establishment Canada (CSEC)
P.O. Box 9703
Ottawa, ON K1G 3Z4
Canada
(613) 991-7248
Web site: http://www.cse-cst.gc.ca
The CSEC, which handles cryptology for the Canadian gov-
ernment, offers links and information on Canadian
antiterrorism and counterterrorism law.

National Consortium for the Study of Terrorism and
Responses to Terrorism (START)
8400 Baltimore Avenue, Suite 250
College Park, MD 20740
(301) 405-6600
Web site: http://www.start.umd.edu/start
START, sponsored by the DHS and located at the University
of Maryland, conducts extensive research in terrorism
and provides numerous research reports on terrorism, as
well as databases and profiles on terrorist organizations.

National Counterterrorism Center (NCTC)
Washington, DC 20511
Web site: http://www.nctc.gov
The NCTC publishes resources like the *Intelligence Guide for First Responders* and the CT Calendar, which offers information on wanted terrorists, terrorist organizations, and ways to identify various terrorist activities.

National Security Agency/Central Security Service
NSA/CSS
Fort Meade, MD 20755-6248
(301) 688-6524
Web site: http://www.nsa.gov
The NSA/CSS works on code breaking and protecting sensitive government information. On the Web site, you can find research about advances in computer and IT technology, and learn about the history of cryptology.

The Stimson Center
1111 19th Street NW
Twelfth Floor
Washington, DC 20036
(202) 223-5956
Web site: http://www.stimson.org
The Stimson Center is a think tank that focuses on peace and security studies. Its Web site provides information and research on a wide variety of issues, from border protection to radiological weapons.

U.S. Department of Homeland Security (DHS)
245 Murray Lane SW
Washington, DC 20528
(202) 282-8000

Web site: http://www.dhs.gov
The DHS provides links and career information about all the
    departments under its control.

U.S. Office of Personnel Management (OPM)
1900 E Street NW
Washington, DC 20415-1000
(202) 606-1800
Web site: http://www.opm.gov
The OPM manages the hiring process for the U.S. govern-
    ment and its agencies. The organization has information
    and resources for everything from student programs to
    evaluations and background investigations.

Web Sites

Due to the changing nature of Internet links, Rosen Publishing
has developed an online list of Web sites related to the
subject of this book. This site is updated regularly. Please use
this link to access the list:

http://www.rosenlinks.com/LAW/ACTF

FOR FURTHER READING

Bergen, Peter. *The Longest War: The Enduring Conflict Between American and Al-Qaeda*. New York, NY: Simon & Schuster, 2011.

Bullock, Jane, et al. *Introduction to Homeland Security: Principals of All-Hazards Response*. Burlington, MA: Elsevier, 2009.

Clarke, Richard A., and Robert Knake. *Cyber Terrorism: The Next Threat to National Security and What to Do About It*. New York, NY: Ecco, 2010.

Coll, Steve. *Ghost Wars: The Secret History of the CIA, Afghanistan, and Bin Laden, from the Soviet Invasion to September 10, 2011*. New York, NY: Penguin, 2004.

Crenshaw, Martha. *Explaining Terrorism: Causes, Processes and Consequences*. New York, NY: Routledge, 2010.

Crumpton, Henry A. *The Art of Intelligence: Lessons from a Life in the CIA's Clandestine Service*. New York, NY: Penguin, 2012.

Deuster, Patricia A., Anita Singh, Pierre A. Pelletier, eds. *The U.S. Navy SEAL Guide to Fitness and Nutrition*. Nashville, TN: BN Publishing, 2011.

Holcomb, Raymond W., and Lillian S. Weiss. *Endless Enemies: Inside FBI Counterterrorism*. Washington, DC: Potomac Books, 2011.

Howard, Russell, and Bruce Hoffman. *Terrorism and Counterterrorism: Understanding the New Security Environment, Readings and Interpretations*. Columbus, OH: McGraw-Hill Education, 2011.

Jensen, Carl J., III, David H. McElreath, and Melissa Graves. *Introduction to Intelligence Studies*. Boca Raton, FL: CRC Press, 2013.

Kraft, Michael, and Edward Marks. *U.S. Government Counterterrorism: A Guide to Who Does What.* Boca Raton, FL: CRC Press, 2012.

Lowenthal, Mark M. *Intelligence: From Secrets to Policy.* 5th ed. Thousand Oaks, CA: CQ Press, 2012.

Mann, Donn, and Ralph Pezullo. *Inside Seal Team Six: My Life and Mission with America's Elite Warriors.* New York, NY: Little, Brown and Company, 2011.

Moore, Steve. *Special Agent Man: My Life in the FBI as a Terrorist Hunter, Helicopter Pilot, and Certified Sniper.* Chicago, IL: Chicago Review Press, 2012.

National Commission on Terrorist Attacks upon the United States. *The 9/11 Commission Report.* New York, NY: W. W. Norton and Company, 2004.

Owen, Mark. *No Easy Day: The Firsthand Account of the Mission that Killed Osama Bin Laden.* New York, NY: Penguin, 2012.

Pichtel, John. *Terrorism and WMDs: Awareness and Response.* Boca Raton, FL: CRC Press, 2011.

Poland, James M. *Understanding Terrorism: Groups, Strategies, and Responses.* 3rd ed. Upper Saddle River, NJ: Prentice Hall, 2010.

Post, Jerrold M. *The Mind of the Terrorist: The Psychology of Terrorism from the IRA to al-Qaeda.* New York, NY: Palgrave Macmillan, 2007.

Shimko, Keith L. *International Relations: Perspectives, Controversies & Readings.* 4th ed. Boston, MA: Wadsworth, 2013.

BIBLIOGRAPHY

Ambinder, Marc. "The Secret Team That Killed Osama bin Laden." Atlantic, May 2, 2011. Retrieved January 2013 (http://www.theatlantic.com/politics/archive/2011/05/the-secret-team-that-killed-osama-bin-laden/238163).

Bureau of Labor Statistics, U.S. Department of Labor. *Occupational Outlook Handbook, 2012-13 Edition.* Retrieved March 23, 2013 (http://www.bls.gov/ooh/military/military-careers.htm).

Central Intelligence Agency. "Career Opportunities." April 11, 2012. Retrieved March 20, 2013 (https://www.cia.gov/careers/opportunities/analytical/counterterrorism-analyst.html).

Central Intelligence Agency. "Student Opportunities." February 21, 2013. Retrieved March 10, 2013 (https://www.cia.gov/careers/student-opportunities/index.html#opp).

Federal Bureau of Investigation. "Careers." www.FBIjobs.gov. Retrieved March 20, 2013 (https://www.fbijobs.gov/11.asp).

Federal Bureau of Investigation. "Protecting America from Terrorist Attack. Meet the National Joint Terrorism Task Force." July 7, 2004. February 20, 2013 (https://www.fbi.gov/news/stories/2004/july/njttf070204).

Federal Bureau of Investigation, U.S. Department of Justice. *Today's FBI: Facts & Figures 2010-2011.* Retrieved January 28, 2013 (http://books.google.com/books?id=xjo4yX6AcklC&printsec=frontcover#v=onepage&q&f=false).

FEMA, U.S. Department of Homeland Security. "Center for Domestic Preparedness Course List." Retrieved March 12, 2013 (https://cdp.dhs.gov/).

Gettleman, Jefferey, Eric Schmitt, and Thom Shanker. "U.S. Swoops In to Free 2 From Pirates in Somali Raid." *New York Times*, January 25, 2012. Retrieved January 2013 (http://www.nytimes.com/2012/01/26/world/africa /us-raid-frees-2-hostages-from-somali-pirates.html?page wanted=1&_r=1&).

Graff, Garrett M. *The Threat Matrix: The FBI at War in the Age of Global Terror*. New York, NY: Little, Brown and Company, 2011.

Hill, Christopher F. "Joint Antiterrorism Doctrine Update." *Guardian Antiterrorism Journal* 13, no. 1 (2011) 7–11.

Hoffman, Bruce. *Inside Terrorism*. New York, NY: Columbia University Press, 2006.

Intelligence.gov "About the Intelligence Community." Retrieved January 6, 2013 (http://intelligence.gov/about-the-intelligence-community/how-intelligence-works.html).

Priest, Dana, and William M. Arkin. *Top Secret America: The Rise of the New American Security State*. New York, NY: Little, Brown and Company, 2011.

Rayment, Sean, and Ben Farmer. "High Praise for Audacious Hostage Rescue." Sydney Morning Herald, June 4, 2012. Retrieved January 2013 (http://www.smh.com. au/world/high-praise-for-audacious-hostage-rescue-20120603-1zq32.html).

Schmidle, Nicholas. "Getting Bin Laden." *New Yorker*, August 8, 2011. Retrieved January 2013 (http://www.newy-orker.com/reporting/2011/08/08/110808fa_fact _schmidle?currentPage=all).

U.S. Department of Defense, Joint Publication. *Department of Defense Dictionary of Military and Associated Terms*. Retrieved January 4, 2013 (http://www.dtic.mil/doctrine/ dod_dictionary).

U.S. Department of Justice. *The Federal Bureau of Investigation's Efforts to Protect the Nation's Seaports (Redacted and Unclassified)*. Retrieved March 4,

2013 (http://www.justice.gov/oig/reports/FBI/a0626
/finings2.htm).

U.S. Department of Justice, Office of the Inspector General.
*The Department of Justice's Terrorism Task Forces
2005*. Retrieved February 3, 2013 (http://www.justice.
gov/oig/reports/plus/e0507).

U.S. Navy. "Navy SEALs (Sea, Air & Land)." Retrieved March
3, 2010 (http://www.navy.com/careers/special-opera-
tions/seals.html).

U.S. Special Operations Command. *Fact Book 2012*.
Retrieved February 17, 2013 (http://www.fas.org/irp
/agency/dod/socom).

A

About the Author

Corinne Grinapol is a writer living in Brooklyn, New York. She is the author of several books for Rosen Publishing. As an international relations major at the State University of New York at Geneseo, she focused on security studies and once considered some of the career options and opportunities detailed in this book.

Photo Credits

Cover Robbin Cresswell/U.S. Air Force; pp. 6–7 (background) clearviewstock /Shutterstock.com; pp. 6–7, 88 Jewel Samad/AFP/Getty Images; pp. 12, 38–39, 46–47, 58, 62, 71, 78–79, 86–87, 94–95, 96–97 © AP Images; pp. 16–17 Mark Wilson/Getty Images; pp. 20–21 Saul Loeb/AFP/Getty Images; pp. 22–23 Paul J.Richards/AFP/Getty Images; pp. 28–29 Staff Sgt. Corey T. Dennis/U.S. Army/AP Images; pp. 34–35 RJ Sangosti /Denver Post/Getty Images; pp. 36–37 Chief Mass Communications Specialist Robert J. Fluegel/U.S. Navy; pp. 42–43 The Washington Post /Getty Images; pp. 48–49 Kim Jae-Hwan/AFP/Getty Images; pp. 52–53 Mario Tama/Getty Images; pp. 64–65 pefostudio5/Shutterstock/com; pp. 74–75 Boston Globe/Getty Images; pp. 82–83 Alan Warren /Newhouse News Service/Landov; p. 84 Rebecca Cook/Reuters/Landov; cover and interior pages background images and textures Alex Gontar /Shutterstock.com; Eky Studio/Shutterstock.com, iStockphoto/Thinkstock, Andreas Liem/Shutterstock.com.

Designer: Michael Moy; Editor: Bethany Bryan;
Photo Editor: Amy Feinberg